Gazing

A Short Book of Poems

Greg Damico

BookLeaf
Publishing

India | USA | UK

Made with ❤ on the BookLeaf Publishing Platform
www.bookleafpub.in
www.bookleafpub.com

Dedication

To my Seattle family, with love and appreciation

Preface

I have been writing songs for quite a long time now. But it's only recently that I have attempted to give the same care to my lyrics that I give to my music. And now here I am, attempting to focus solely on words. Perhaps I'll set some of these to music one day, but that is really the furthest thing from my mind at the moment.

I just want, rather, to try to say something about what's in my heart. The idea of *gazing* has many connotations, but I was thinking about my own nature as both a navel-gazer and a stargazer, and I was thinking also of how often good art is simply a matter of *observing*, of looking, of gazing at the world and reporting what one sees. And so indeed these poems are the result of my *gazing*: at the world, at others, at myself. I hope by them to encourage others to do the same.

Acknowledgements

Even if some of us have more natural talent than others, I suppose no one is born with a great ability to write. And many of us have also a natural aversion, no doubt the result of evolutionary selection over a long period of differential pressures, to sharing their creations once made.

And so it strikes me that my acknowledgments must be to two sorts of people: to those who helped me develop whatever facility I have with words, and also to those who helped me develop the confidence to make my thoughts public.

My parents surely belong to both groups, and they are not the only ones who do.

Writing well begins with the appreciation of language as such for its power and beauty, and the list of those who've nurtured that in me is quite long indeed. But I'd like at least to mention my brother, Gary; my high school teacher, Brinda Price; and one of my intellectual heroes, Douglas Hofstadter.

Graduate school in philosophy involved being in a

community full of writers and critics, constantly reading each other's work, offering friendly criticisms or enthusiastic endorsements. That sort of environment is invaluable for inspiring confidence in one's own work, and again the list of members of that community would be too long to go through in detail. But I'd like to recognize Adam Sennet, Elaine Landry, and the late John Malcolm for their unwavering encouragement.

1. Misunderstanding

You wanted to talk, but I didn't want to listen
About how the common can mutate into the cruel.
It's curious how normal the painful can honestly be,
And strange how we could have avoided it all.

At times all we need is a touch or a look of concern.
In moments like that one you simply desired that I hear
you.
I see this all now, and I realize how I came off.
But now is not then and where we are now I don't know.

2. I love it when you play that song by Jackie Greene

I love it when you play that song by Jackie Greene;
I'm sure that you must know by now the one I mean?

It's sad and warm, familiar like a scar.
Lamenting people, drinking at the bar.

So full of thoughts, what might have been,
Atoning not for Sunday's sin.

I feel as though I'm there,
Like living on a dare,

The subject peers
Between his ears

For peace
Release

3. Sleeping in

Huddled, cuddled, warm beneath the blanket,
Solving puzzles, sussing out the Wordle.

Work to do but that can wait a minute–
Comfort's here between my sheet and pillow.

Thinking in my rev'rie 'bout my schedule,
Here and there a mental note or two. It's

Going to be a good, productive day as
Soon as I decide I will begin it.

4. Allen

Well we used to ask Allen what he wanted to be
When he grew up and he would say that he wanted to be
beautiful.
We jeered him, then, for being so superficial.
We'd say, "Not everyone can be beautiful, Allen," and he'd
agree.

Sure, we kept on asking him but his answer would never
change.
He was aiming for beauty and that was that.
We started to wonder if maybe he didn't understand our
question.
Or maybe it was we who didn't understand his answer?

Allen wasn't one of those Christians but he said he'd read
about Jesus.
He liked to say that the real miracle was not so much
Jesus's divinity
But rather his humanity. Now *that* was an
Appropriate object of veneration, he used to say.

Well Allen has reached adulthood now and he's got a
wife and kids and bills and a mortgage.
He looks his age: He's puffy around the eyes and around

his middle.

He's got weak knees and a bad back and a humdinger of a scar on his cheek.

He's frequently tired and sometimes absent-minded, and he'll talk your ear off if you let him.

But we sure do all love him and enjoy him and think he's a good dad and husband.

The last time I went to see him he made me a bowl of soup and let me talk about my problems.

The other day someone asked me what I thought Allen was doing with his life,

And I said I reckon he's doing what he wants to do.

5. Life lessons

Remember:

When your pa says, "I need an extra hand,"
He's not wishing for polydactyly.
When the yogi says, "exhale",
She doesn't mean it rectally.

A sign that says "Slow Children"
Is not necessarily where the short bus stops.
And if a friend cuts off a mattress tag
That's no reason to call the cops.

"Wet Paint" and "Wet Floor"
Are not in the imperative mood,
And if you ever find road apples,
They're not a source of food.

Ant colonies and penal colonies do not have the same
deep structure
Despite a superficial similarity
And politicians are sometimes serious
In spite of their hilarity.

Though some will say it's prescriptive

Lexicography's descriptive
And what's called a theory in science
Can be trusted with reliance.

6. English lessons

If I'm detained I'm in detention
But what's maintained is not in maintention
And my contentions have rather little to do
With what I've successfully contained.

What pertains hereto is pertinent
Thus what we've attained is attinent
If from these lessons there's nothing in us retinent
From such words let's choose just to be abstinent.

Now what repels is repellent
Just as what propels is propellent
But what excels is excellent
And what compels is compulsory.

How easy it should very well be
In attempting such confusion to dispel
To get a form quite wrong indeed
And thus some word misspell!

7. New bar

My ordinary haunt was closed the other day
And so I wandered to a bar unknown to me.

I got to chatting with the barman over bourbon;
We talked about sports and weather and politics.

He asked if I had kids and I said that I did not.
I asked him then about his own.

He sighed and said that he had three.
I said that that was great and wonderful.

He laughed and said "You're OK, kid"
And then he poured me one for free.

I've thought a lot about that sigh
And wondered how I ought to take it.

But the next time I went out for a drink
My old place had opened up again.

8. Forty thousand pin pricks on my lungs

I figure I've probably smoked about 200 cartons of
cigarettes
And though it's been many years since I had my last
I still wonder about the forty thousand pin pricks on my
lungs.

Forty thousand accompaniments of life's little episodes,
Upon waking up or after dining, or burning one
postcoitally,
A complement to coffee or to booze, something to do
while waiting for a train.

Other times the act was more purposeful,
Like trying to calm myself down before or after
something stressful,
Perhaps giving a big lecture or sharing grievous news.

Sometimes simply looking cool was my main motivation,
Or trying to fit in in a group of smoking friends.
The excuses were varied and numerous.

But in time none of those excuses really moved me
anymore.

Perhaps I started thinking more about my health or
getting older,
Or perhaps I merely said that I don't need these
anymore.

I'm sure my lungs must be fairly pink again by now, even
though those cigarettes
Scarred me and put me at greater risk for various
maladies.
But even so it's true that every now and then I miss
them, and they tempt me once again.

9. What we are

Joe Quinn told me he's Irish
Even though he's born in Cleveland
He said his gran's a Dubliner
And that the Quinns go back many years.

Joe said he'd just been studying
His own family tree
And that "where he'd been" would tell him
Where soon he'd likely be.

He's started to take his genes
As an explanation for
The many features of
His complex personality.

That's why I'm irascible! he says,
And why I like to drink.
It's why I can't abandon my faith
And why I hate the Brits.

It's why I love the great outdoors
And why I wear the color green
It's why I love my leprechauns
And give my Gaelic screeds.

Sometimes I criticize Joe Quinn
For something that he's doing.
If he could help it then he would, he says,
But he's a prisoner of his heritage.

And then he goes on the offensive,
Saying I'm insensitive to the Irish
But I say that the stereotypes
Are coming all from his side.

What about the Irish who aren't irascible, I say
And the ones who never drink?
What about the atheistic ones
And those who love the Brits?

What about the homebody Irish
And the ones who hate the color green?
The ones who hate their leprechauns
And keep their Gaelic to themselves?

It seems to me that Joe wants help
In deciding who he is.
He wants to be a member
Of a certain sort of club.

For the things he likes about himself

He wants to feel community
And for the things he doesn't like
He wants them all excused.

I do think he's a prisoner
Of his lovely Irish heritage
But it seems to me he's jailor too
If you can see, then, what I mean.

10. The outsider

OK, my name you can't pronounce and I'm from a long
way from here
But I have some thoughts about you people if you'll
permit me, if you'll hear
I don't understand the things and goals that some of you
hold dear
But if you give me a few minutes then I'll try to make it
clear.

Mostly I don't understand why more of you don't read!
The books and libraries you have are the greatest thing
I've see'd
I get that y'all must start off from a place of basic need,
But once you're fed and watered then it's time for books
indeed!

I'll be the first to grant you: television has its time,
But exercising not your reading muscles is a crime!
So walk and stretch and move to keep your body in its
prime,
But then you must surround yourself in narratives
sublime.

And one more thing I'd like to say that can no longer

wait:

Why can't we love our differences instead of feeling
hate?
Your neighbors live their lives in fashions other than
your own,
But surely that won't mean that they aren't made of flesh
and bone?

11. Some things take two hands to wield

Some things take two hands to wield and some things only one.
Other things demand a strength that most of us don't know.

Guitars take two, a pen takes one, but what about a view
That challenges and makes us think and forces us to grow?

Some things take two hands to wield and some things only one.
Other things require a fit and hale imagination.

A broom takes two, and chopsticks one; solutions to our ills
Need certain faculties of thought and never mind your phys'cal station.

Some things take two hands to wield and some things only one
But all the most important things require no hands at all.

One needn't have a hand to care or love or make a

difference

Nor need you one to hold a friend and thus prevent their fall.

12. They're marching to the rhythm of the drum

They're coming and they're marching and they're angry as hell.
They want their representatives to do their jobs well.

And they're marching to the beat of the rum-pum-pum
And they're marching to the rhythm of the drum.

They say the weak need our protection and that's why we have a State
And if we give up on them that will inspire only hate

And they're marching to the beat of the rum-pum-pum
And they're marching to the rhythm of the drum.

They want to feel protected when they're weak and infirm
And those who are a threat to that won't get another term

And they're marching to the beat of the rum-pum-pum
And they're marching to the rhythm of the drum.

Why should billionaires get richer and the poor get less?

They fear civil society they've turned into a mess!

And they're marching to the beat of the rum-pum-pum
And they're marching to the rhythm of the drum.

They've heard only broken promises and bald-faced lies
What happened to our values? Now come look us in the
eyes!

And they're marching to the beat of the rum-pum-pum
And they're marching to the rhythm of the drum.

Who cares about a businessman who's made a bunch of
dough?
If he hasn't helped society then he had better go!

And they're marching to the beat of the rum-pum-pum
And they're marching to the rhythm of the drum.

It's our schools and our hospitals, our prisons and our
old
We measure our success rate by who's left out in the
cold.

And they're marching to the beat of the rum-pum-pum
And they're marching to the rhythm of the drum.

13. All my many things

All my many things are like a flock of different birds.
Many things are albatrosses or other things absurd.

But others have a time and place, and value in my heart,
I'll try now to describe them, at least to make a start.

My books are like my penguins, keeping warm my
thoughts,
In a huddled mass of feathers, all the things that I've
been taught.

Guitars are like my mockingbird, singing out with art,
Sometimes imitating those who move its little heart.

My clothes comprise a motley crew: restraint and
ostentation,
The ones like wrens, the rest a peacock in its excitation.

My cups and bowls are cuckoo birds, reminding me to
have a bite,
My bed a lovely nightingale, seducing me at night.

My vacuum is a vulture, devouring whatever's at its feet,
While my mirror's like a parrot, knowing only to repeat.

My best ideas hummingbirds flitting out of sight,
But your love is like an owl hunting noiselessly at night.

14. Speaking out

Once there was a man residing in a free land.
An ally of that land was once attacked, and
That ally, with superior military prowess,
Set to running counterstrikes for months' time I confess.

The free man felt the ally was clearly overstepping,
though
There may have been some punishment a little more
befitting,
But now the death, destruction from the
counteroffensive
Had proven than the starting strike even more
expensive.

Demonstrate, protest, and then make your voice heard!
That's how he opted to respond to this felt wrong: with
words.
I'm sure he must have felt then that he would have
protection
It's a glorious thing indeed to get to live without
inspection.

Instead the government's forces have put him in
detention.

They've threatened to deport him just for giving his view
a mention.
And many felt the free land was clearly overstepping.
Was there even any punishment that we would call
befitting?

Demonstrate, protest, and then make your voice heard!
That's how I've opted to respond to this felt wrong: with
words.

15. Injustice detector

There's a little part of me that mostly keeps its mouth
shut.
But it's stirred by callousness and inhumanity.
Sometimes it won't speak about a minuscule
transgression,
But it watches and remembers and it has a breaking
point.

There's fairness and unfairness, there's what's just and
unjust,
And though they neither can be seen we're not
unsensing of either.
And when I see some gross injustice, this little part of me
takes a little invisible Polaroid,
So then I'll recognize the perpetrator if and when they
come around again.

My collection of invisible Polaroids depicts mostly small
and petty things.
A greedy man pushing to the front of a line, that sort of
malfeasance.
But at the end of this long string of photographs I saw
something unexpected.

There it was, undeniable, a Polaroid of yours truly, still keeping his mouth shut.

16. I like to walk in new landscapes

I like to walk in new landscapes
Where there's sun and water
And the sun hits the water just right–
Bang! you can feel like a new person

Or like you want to be a new person
Or like a new beautiful person is about
To reveal itself if only your old and ugly self
Would just get out of the way already!

Sometimes the breeze can just set you thinking
About life and what's important
And sometimes there's nothing more important
Than that breeze that got you thinking.

The air is wet and warm and salty and delicious
And the sand caresses your feet as though you
Had placed them into one of those screens with all the
little pins
That form the shape of whatever impresses them

And so your feet are impressed but really your whole
body is too

And come to think of it *you* are impressed by the whole experience
And sometimes everything just feels like it's going to be OK
And all you have to do is just to keep doing what you're doing.

Other times you're walking on grass or wood or pavement
And maybe this time it's chilly and cloudy
But still the chill can be invigorating
And maybe there are woodland sounds

Or in some other way you're really vibing with the scenery
And you feel like you're part of it but also somehow bigger than it
And at the same time smaller too. It doesn't really make sense
But also in that moment everything that matters really does seem to make sense.

Sometimes I think it's just that my body is happy
Because I'm outside using it and getting some exercise.
But there are these other special times that I'm trying to describe
Where there's something else happening.

It's psychological and emotional and maybe even
spiritual
And there's some kind of love or power or force
That makes you feel connected with things.
I like to walk in new landscapes.

17. To have loved and lost

Well my dad was trying to console me the other day.
You see, I had just had a romantic relationship dry up.

It was all pretty unexpected and I wasn't feeling too
great about it
And I reckon he took it upon himself to set to cheering
me up.

He said, Well you know they don't say that it's *less
painful*
To have loved and lost than never to have loved at all.

And they don't say that it's *more fun* or that loving and
losing
Is *more interesting* or *more satisfying* or anything like
that.

If we compare loving and losing with never having loved
The former doesn't come out ahead in terms of being

More pleasant or more beautiful or happier or more
entertaining
Or sexier or more virtuous or more attractive or less
miserable.

But still it's better, son. They just say that it's better,
And I reckon that they're right.

And even if loving and losing, when compared to never loving,
Is in fact *more painful* and *less fun* and *less interesting*
and *less satisfying*,

And even if it's *less pleasant* and *less beautiful* and *less
happy* and *less entertaining*,
Less sexy and *less virtuous* and *less attractive* and *more
miserable*,

Still it's better. It's better. Still I think it's better.

18. Everyone is waiting for love

It seems that everyone is waiting for love.

Little children everywhere are waiting to be grown,
And widowers and widows anticipate reunions.
My aunt Maisie has been waiting for forty-seven years
And, Lord, there are so many who are crying in their
beers.

How strange it is that all of us, no matter our success,
Should feel this need, this lack, rather deep inside of us.
The thirty-somethings talk about it, and sometimes also
read
About romantic exploits of the lucky ones indeed.

The forty-somethings turn to art and contemplate their
fate,
While fifty-somethings put on films from many years
ago.
The elderly, who ought by now to've had their fill of
waiting,
Still sit and wait for love, indeed they've learned to love
the waiting!

Now it's true that some have given up and closed
themselves to love,
And some content themselves with wishes of riches from
above.
But if deep down you ask them of what it is they feel,
I think most of them will own that it's love that gives
them zeal.

It seems that everyone is waiting for love.

19. On being afraid

Sometimes when I ask people whether they might do
some bold thing,
They say that they're afraid to do it, as if that settled the
matter.

Yes, yes, of course you're afraid, I say. It would hardly be
the bold thing if you weren't.
But how you respond to that fear, well, that's the heart of
the matter.

Let us act for reasons and not let our passions rule us!
We can all read Kant and then agree to let his thinking
school us.

Feeling fear should never mean that that option's
unavailable.
And courage is not lack of fear -- this logic's
unassailable!

But courage rather will involve the staring down of fear
And acting on the values that one holds forever dear.

Now let's proceed with caution lest we overstate the
case,

For sometimes fear's a sign that one had best give up the
chase.

Courage is a virtue, but one ought also to be prudent
So listen to your heart and of discretion be a student.

At times the best advice is just to wait another day
But other times you've got to fight and fight on come
what may.

20. Data science

Data descriptions and data encryptions,
Columns and rows and tables and views,
Scraping a website in total compliance:
These are all part of the new data science.

Exploring correlations and trait engineering,
New models and new comprehension are nearing,
Include as predictor the launch angle theta:
These are all part of the science of data.

Running a test on a favored hypothesis,
Announcing your alpha rate as a parenthesis,
Remember that power is 1 - beta:
These are all part of the science of data.

Machine learning models for class or regression,
Let's use SKLearn to give it expression,
Looking for 90% recall or greater:
These are all part of the science of data.

Trying cross-entropy loss and the hinge,
Limiting variance with Lasso and Ridge,
Turning to wrappers for systems' alliance:
These are all part of the new data science.

Deep neural networks and robust AI,
Large language models in the blink of an eye
Creating and working in our senses' defiance:
These, too, are part of the new data science.

21. Society

There's the story of the man who was interpreter of
Persian,
Who liked to mistranslate despite Iranian immersion.
He claimed that he was culpable for much
miscommunication,
Some of which had nearly led to war between the
nations.

And then there is the doctor who misprescribed with
malice.
A certain patient ended up in hospital in Dallas.
It seems that deep inside she had a wicked sense of
humor,
Anyway, as I recall, that was the common rumor.

Again there is the traffic cop who gave out tickets
randomly,
And many honest motorists were trapped and then fined
handsomely.
Once again there was no satisfying explanation,
And all the common people were beset by consternation.

I mention these vignettes because we're mothers and
we're brothers,

And our society is frail and we depend upon each other.
Most members of humanity are as strangers on a bus,
But ultimately most of them are really just like us.